W9-CKM-094

Back and Forth

by Lola M. Schaefer

Consulting Editor: Gail Saunders-Smith, Ph.D.

Consultant: P. W. Hammer, Ph.D., Acting Manager of Education, American Institute of Physics

Pebble Books

an imprint of Capstone Press
Mankato, Minnesota

Pebble Books are published by Capstone Press
818 North Willow Street, Mankato, Minnesota 56001
http://www.capstone-press.com

Library of Congress Cataloging-in-Publication Data
Schaefer, Lola M., 1950–
    Back and forth/by Lola M. Schaefer.
    p. cm.—(The way things move)
    Includes bibliographical references and index.
    Summary: Simple text and photographs provide examples of back-and-forth
movement, including the pendulum in a clock, a child in a rocking chair, and a tree
in the wind.
    ISBN 0-7368-0398-X
    1. Oscillations—Juvenile literature. [1. Motion.] I. Title. II. Series.
QA865.S33   2000
531'.32—dc21   99-18303
                                                                                CIP

Note to Parents and Teachers

The series The Way Things Move supports national science standards for units on understanding motion and the principles that explain it. The series also shows that things move in many different ways. This book describes and illustrates back-and-forth movement. The photographs support early readers in understanding the text. The repetition of words and phrases helps early readers learn new words. This book also introduces early readers to subject-specific vocabulary words, which are defined in the Words to Know section. Early readers may need assistance to read some words and to use the Table of Contents, Words to Know, Read More, Internet Sites, and Index/Word List sections of the book.

Table of Contents

Back and forth is
movement backward
and forward.

Arms move
back and forth.

Eyes move
back and forth.

A rolling pin moves back and forth.

Tree branches move
back and forth.

A chair rocks
back and forth.

Waves flow
back and forth.

pendulum

18

A pendulum swings back and forth.

A ball bounces
back and forth.

Words to Know

backward—to the back

forward—to the front

movement—the act of changing position from place to place

pendulum—a weight that hangs in a clock; a pendulum moves back and forth to help the clock keep time.

rolling pin—a tube-shaped kitchen tool used to flatten dough

Read More

Canizares, Susan and Betsey Chessen. *Make It Move!* Science Emergent Readers. New York: Scholastic, 1999.

Oxlade, Christopher. *Energy and Movement.* Step-by-Step Science. New York: Children's Press, 1998.

White, Laurence B. *Energy: Simple Experiments for Young Scientists.* Brookfield, Conn.: Millbrook Press, 1995.

Internet Sites

Amusement Park Physics—Pendulum
http://www.learner.org/exhibits/parkphysics/pendulum.html

Home Experiments
http://scifun.chem.wisc.edu/HOMEEXPTS/HOMEEXPTS.html

Reeko's Mad Scientist Lab
http://www.flash.net/~spartech/ReekoScience/MoreExperimentsSortCategory.htm

Index/Word List

Word Count: 54
Early-Intervention Level: 6

Editorial Credits
Martha E. H. Rustad, editor; Timothy Halldin, cover designer; Heidi Schoof, photo researcher

Photo Credits
David F. Clobes, 8, 14
Heidi Schoof, 10
James L. Shaffer, 6
Photo Network/Rene Laursen, 16
Photophile/Bachmann, 20
Tom Stack/TOM STACK & ASSOCIATES, 12
Uniphoto, cover, 1; Uniphoto/Lew Lause, 18
Visuals Unlimited/Arthur R. Hill, 4